CW00694967

HOW TO SAVE YOUR RELATIONSHIP
...From Yourself

A Myth-Busting Guide
To Successful Love

Melissa Smith Baker

How To Save Your Relationship... From Yourself
A Myth-Busting Guide to Successful Love

Copyright © 2013 by Melissa Smith Baker

ISBN 978-1-939812-06-3
Sebastopol, CA

Find out more about Melissa Smith Baker and upcoming books online at **www.lovingforkeeps.com**

ACKNOWLEDGEMENTS

I would never have written this book if it weren't ₁ ₁ my husband, Chris. We've been a couple through thick and thin for over 37 years, and Chris is my greatest and most beloved teacher.

It takes a village to create a book. I would like to express my heartfelt thanks to Theresa Dintino, my above-and-beyond writing buddy, to Mary Ellen Baker, my creative web developer, to Therese Mughannam-Walrath and David Walrath, my friends whom I can always count on, to Cris Wanzer, my editor extraordinaire, to Stephen Hutchins, my gracious book designer, and to my supportive marriage and women's groups, friends, relatives, and students.

This book would never have happened without each and every one of you – and I'm not exaggerating!

Also, thank you to Cathy Thorne, the imaginative cartoonist on my website, **www.lovingforkeeps.com**, and on the cover of this book. Her cartoons help couples remember that humor and fun are also part of long-term relationships.

DEDICATION

- TABLE OF CONTENTS -

INTRODUCTION

In this small but mighty book, I bust 31 deadly relationship myths. Myths are fictional stories that humans have heard over and over again and have integrated into their thinking, as if they were true, to explain things that they don't understand — in this case, the mystery of committed relationships.

Many of these beliefs have been deeply engrained in our human psyche for millennia. That's one of the reasons why they are so difficult to extricate and eradicate. Discovering and revealing the truth by busting these myths will pave the way to creating thriving and deeply fulfilling long-term relationships.

Why a story?

Scattered throughout the book are stories that help illustrate a myth concept. These examples will be more impactful to you if you don't just think about them as stories about someone else's life. Maybe you haven't experienced the exact same thing, but on some level at some time in your life, you've probably had a variation-on-a-theme experience. Place yourself in these stories as much as you can, otherwise you won't get the full benefit from these vignettes. What does the story mean to you? What does the story say about who you are and how you see your own life and relationship?

How to read this book

Resist the temptation to read this book from cover to cover in one sitting. Read one myth then stop. The goal is to contemplate each myth, to see how it is playing out in your relationship, to imagine stepping beyond the myth to a new freedom, and then to integrate this new thinking into your life. You won't be able to attain this goal unless you take one myth at a time and reflect on it. It is often helpful to discuss these myths in a group, though it is not mandatory. Gather some friends and your partner, if she or he wants to participate. (You can be part of a group even if your partner doesn't want to.) What is essential, however, is doing the exercises, reflecting, and taking action to change your life.

If you need help, please contact me: mel@lovingforkeeps.com. I'd be thrilled to see relationship myth-busting groups proliferate throughout the world, and I'd be delighted to help you set up your demythologizing group — for free. I am a relationship trainer, and I derive great pleasure from helping people learn how to love and be loved.

Your myth-busting tour starts now. Enjoy the exhilaration, liberation and empowerment of debunking the following 31 relationship myths.

THE SOUL MATE MYTH

If I find my soul mate, I'll have a great relationship.

Most people believe in soul mates.

No matter the spiritual, religious, or secular belief system, humans invariably ask the same questions about relationships: How do I know I've found the right partner? How can I be sure that I'm with THE ONE, the one and only for me? Am I with Mr. Right? Or, is she Ms. Wrong?

Couples contemplate these questions, whether they're old or young, at the beginning of their relationships, or even after 30 years of being together.

Perhaps the soul mate myth is an attempt to understand the mystery of two people falling in love. Unfortunately, there's no formula to determine the chemistry and long-term compatibility of any couple. Some of the most unlikely duos have prospered and endured, while other pairs with shared interests, culture, and backgrounds have floundered, crashed, and burned.

The good news is this: While falling in love can't be figured out, cultivating a successful, long-lasting relationship that survives the thick and thin of life can be.

First of all, ask yourself what a soul mate means to you. Does it mean you're never disappointed with your partner? Does it mean your partner always says the right thing at the right time? Does it mean your partner can read your mind and anticipate your needs?

What you believe about the soul mate question is crucial to your long-term relationship happiness.

One of my students said what a soul mate meant to her: Someone who would understand her on every level — body, mind and soul and always accept every part of her. Really? Can any partner ever live up to this overly idealized definition? Can you? If your definition is similar, your relationship could be doomed to fail.

The soul mate notion is tricky to disabuse yourself of. You have to be vigilant because this myth is perpetuated in novels and the media cross-culturally.

We shouldn't believe writers of fiction and fairy tales. But we do! They are not our relationship teachers, yet we allow them to be. The entertainment industry, no matter how much we enjoy it or how much it comforts us, is not reality.

Story

One of my students told me that for him and his wife, it was love at first sight. They knew unequivocally that they were soul mates. Since they were both astrologers, they planned their wedding day to fall on the right configuration of stars and planets. More than a decade later, however, they ended up going through an acrimonious divorce. How could this happen?

Tragically, couples split up more often than necessary. Many marriages have everything going for them, but what they lack is an understanding of reality-based relationship dynamics. Setting yourself free from the burden of the soul mate myth is important to your relationship's longevity and happiness.

Let's take a close look at the soul mate myth and bust it once and for all.

Busted Myth

Believing in Prince Charming and Cinderella will not make you happy. It will actually contribute to your long-term relationship dissatisfaction and discontentment. Here are a few of the reasons why —

1. The quest for a soul mate deludes you into thinking that there must be someone better out there than your current partner, someone who would make you happier if you could only find her or him.

2. Without the ironclad soul mate guarantee, you might feel that your chances for happiness are non-existent. Unfortunately, the truth is you can never know beyond a shadow of a doubt whether you've found or haven't found your soul mate.

3. If you believe that you and your soul mate partner are so in tune with each other, you might end up taking your relationship for granted. This could lead you into thinking that there is no

need to nourish your soul mate union because it's already and always perfect. This is a recipe for certain disaster.

The soul mate ideal is a powerful illusion that resists being easily dispelled. Most of us accept this myth to greater or lesser degrees. We can, however, through our own inner work, grow up and reconcile our childhood fantasies with a mature point of view of love and romance based in reality. From there we can experience a real relationship that is more amazing than dreams of knights in shining armor and damsels in distress.

Contrary to popular belief, soul mates are not found; they are made. If you've been with the same partner for a long time, then chances are you've already chosen Mr. or Ms. Right, but you may have lost sight of it because of the natural forces working inside your long-term relationship.

If you did a poll of divorced couples, you'd discover that many of them thought they were "soul mates" in the beginning of their relationship. Being soul mates did not prevent them from being unhappy or getting divorced, and it will not stop that from happening to you, either.

Or, perhaps you are like other couples that feel they are married to the "wrong" person. Maybe you felt you had to marry because you got pregnant, or there was some other extenuating circumstance. It doesn't matter.

What matters is this: Getting rid of the soul mate myth allows you to begin to see the real you and to see the real person that is your partner. And, surprisingly, once you unburden yourself, both you and your partner can become true "soul mates," to yourselves and to each other. You are your own soul mate, the one you've been looking for, and your partner is the one you have been hoping to find. In this way, soul mates are created, capable of facing the trials, tribulations, and jubilations of a long-term relationship while sharing a deeply connected intimacy along the way. What could be more fulfilling?

Begin the journey. Bust the soul mate myth in yourself.

Your myth-busting tour continues. Enjoy the exhilaration, liberation and empowerment of debunking relationship myths.

THE COMMITMENT MYTH

Being in a long-term relationship, and not in one, is possible.

Why are commitments so difficult?

Humans, be they in a committed relationship or single, feel uncomfortable making choices. Although some decisions are small (i.e., buying new towels) and others big (i.e., getting married), most people try to avoid making a commitment unless up against the wall.

This is because with every choice there is loss. That's the nature of choice and commitment. Do you have the courage to face your fears about the uncertainty of your choices as well as missing out on what you didn't choose? Once you've closed the door to the possibility of "all opportunities are open," you might panic, allowing indulgent thoughts of "What if?" or "Why didn't I?" to keep nagging at you. Can you accept the facts that life has no certainties, and it's impossible to do and be everything?

The reality is that you can have anything you choose, but you can only choose one thing at a time. Your life can only proceed along a single path.

A monogamous, long-term relationship challenges the fantasy that you can have it all, but the truth is you couldn't have it all when you were single, either. Having it all is an illusion. Inherent in decision-making is not having it all. It might be upsetting having to give up this belief, but keeping it is destructive to your personal integrity.

Why is your integrity involved in commitment? Because that's how you make decisions, from who you are, what you value, and what's meaningful to you. If you could do anything at anytime and no decisions really mattered, you wouldn't be able to define yourself.

Surprisingly, commitment makes you free, not limited, if you understand that the definition of freedom isn't about doing anything you want at any time — rather, it is about becoming more of who you are.

Maybe you've become bad at decision-making because of a consumer "return policy" mentality. Shopping and the media may have seduced you into thinking that no commitments need ever be made.

Even after decades of marriage, you may still be thinking that you haven't married the right person. Do you think that if you could make a partner exchange, your life would be better? How long does the "money-back guarantee" have to last in order for you to feel assured of a decision? Obviously, in relationships, no length of time will ever suffice. In every commitment, there is always an emotional price to pay. Commitments are not pure and simple. They are choices between one anxiety and another, doing something or not doing something, gaining something or losing something — either path is filled with fears, pros and cons, consequences, and no guarantees. This is why decisions, commitments, and choices are so difficult, yet they are the key to determining the quality of the life you live. And they are essential to the quality of your relationship with your partner.

Busted Myth

Having one foot in and one foot out of a relationship is self-protection that doesn't work. Statements such as, "I never really committed to my partner anyway, so she or he can't hurt me," are testaments to your inability to commit to yourself and to love another real human being. It may seem safer emotionally to act this way, but this cover-all-bases-just-in-case philosophy promotes what you likely fear most — relationship dysfunction, not health.

The more you commit to yourself on a daily basis, the greater ability you'll have to commit to your partner. Do you do what you say you'll do? Do you show up for yourself, for what you say you'd like to do and be? Commitment is ultimately about you and about who you are.

"Commitment," which is decision making, isn't a dirty word, something to avoid. As Goethe said, "Until one is committed, there is hesitancy, the choice to draw back, always ineffec-tiveness…the moment one definitely commits oneself…all sorts of things occur to help one that would never otherwise have occurred."

Even though you'd like to have many, you only get one choice at a time. If you decide to be in a monogamous relationship, then that's what you have to practice. You can't be married and not married at the same time, but that is what many people are desperately trying to be, regardless of whether an affair is involved or not.

Have you consciously committed to your partner? You might be surprised to know that a commitment ambiguity is part of many relationships, even couples who have been together for a long time. Sitting on the fence and not making commitments is a destabilizing position that will never make you or your relationship happy and will never lead to the deep intimacy you desire.

Take the risk of committing to your partner — not just when you get engaged and on your wedding day, but on a regular basis. Commit to the relationship with yourself, too. It's not easy; but, if you go the whole nine yards, you'll never regret having committed to yourself and to your partner, even if you don't stay together.

Realize that you have made a choice to be in your relationship and that every choice causes anxiety and second thoughts. Once you commit, the doubts and second thoughts that inevitably come up become doorways to growth, deeper satisfaction and connection within your relationship.

Your myth-busting tour continues. Enjoy the exhilaration, liberation and empowerment of debunking relationship myths.

THE STRESS AND ANXIETY MYTH

Having anxieties is a psychological disorder.

Stress is a ubiquitous emotion that everyone can relate to. Who doesn't talk about how they need relief from stress?

Varying levels of stress operate in humans all of the time. This is normal, part of the human condition. Humans are more or less uneasy creatures. Being aware of this fact is key to promoting health in all relationships, especially the one with yourself and with your partner.

What is stress?

Here are its aliases: worry, upset, uneasiness, fear, unsettled feelings, feelings of intensity, nervousness, anxiety, etc. Stress is a synonym and encompasses all of these. Each anxious emotion produces the same thing — a disturbance to your sense of balance and well-being.

Here is the bad news: There are periods of higher and lower stress levels in your life, but you can't ever completely get rid of it. Here is the good news: Even though you can't eradicate stress from your human experience, you can do something each time it prevents you from living your life to the fullest.

How do you know you're stressed?

You can feel it in your body — a queasy stomach, a mind spinning with too many thoughts, a racing heartbeat, sweaty palms, an overall sense of uneasiness. You can notice it in your communication — talking too fast, too much, or in high-pitched tones, not listening to what others are saying, getting defensive, or not being able to sit still.

Everyone has their own somatic patterns, which then translate into coping mechanisms. What are yours? After you feel not quite right, do you eat too much or too little, withdraw, or over-extend yourself? Or, do you take a walk or meditate? Do you lash out at your partner?

If you are jealous or angry or depressed, anxiety (uneasiness) underlies these emotions. Since anxiety is the biggest all-encompassing force that exists in your life and consequently in your relationship, it is absolutely imperative that you know how to settle yourself down, that you know ways to control your stress and bring it down to a level that you can tolerate. Anxiety is not a disorder; it's part of life for every human on the planet.

Exercise

Everyone has unique ways of bringing balance to her or his inner world, the only world capable of being controlled. Different people can tolerate varying levels of stress. What stresses one person, doesn't stress another.

Once you recognize when you're off balance, here's what you can do: Slow down your breathing. Being aware of your breath helps integrate your body, mind, and inner self, allowing you to stay focused on the present, not the past or the future.

Stop talking, or whatever you are doing. Sit or lie down and close your eyes. Focus on your breath — not on anything or anyone else. Inflate your belly with the inhalation as you slowly count to 3. Hold your breath for 3 counts. Then exhale as you count to 3. Repeat this exercise for three or more rounds.

If you're in a situation where you can't lie or sit down for a couple of minutes, stand and do the same exercise. You don't even have to close your eyes, just breathe deeply. It will automatically ground you. Try it right now. You will feel a difference immediately.

Beyond slowing and deepening your breath (which oxygenates the body and brain), eating properly, and getting enough sleep and exercise, you'll have to figure out what's best for you to do in order to maintain your own equilibrium.

Here's a way to help you identify stress strategies that are idiosyncratic to you –

Create a custom-made list of what you love to do. It'll be a different list for everyone. Maybe it's singing Irish songs, painting abstract designs, line dancing, meditating outside, writing poetry about nature, reading books, etc. Refer often to your list of specific things that you enjoy, and do whatever it takes to be in balance. (Getting drunk, doing drugs, raging, etc. are not effective forms of stress relief.)

23

Make your list long. When you're out of sorts, you won't want to do much to get yourself out of your doldrums. If you've written down many things, it'll be more likely that you'll choose at least one thing on your list that you're willing to do.

If you can't calm yourself down in healthy ways, you can't connect with your inner self or anybody else.

🌿 🌿 🌿

Anxiety is a driving force in everyone's life. It determines what you do and don't do. Paradoxically, however, stress actually helps you learn. Stress often gets a bad rap, but it does have a positive function and is necessary. It gets you up in the morning to start doing something and infuses your creative pursuits and achievements with excitement and enthusiasm.

If your education hadn't stressed you, you wouldn't have progressed, and if it stressed you too much or too little, it was damaging to your development. What's the happy stress medium? That's why the goal is not stress eradication, never going beyond your comfort zone, but management. When stress rises, direct it to be a positive, not a destructive force in your life – and determine how much stress-challenge you need and don't need to keep your life and relationship moving forward.

Busted Myth

If you are human, you are anxious. Every human being has anxieties and fears, even if they appear that they don't. Don't be fooled. Even the most handled person on the outside has anxiety happening on the inside. Being alive and asking existential questions that have no absolute answers can drive people crazy. We all live in varying degrees of anxious states all of the time. "What if this happens?" "What if that happens?" we ask ourselves. There are no definitive answers to most of our questions.

Couples are experts at tossing their stress back and forth to each other like a hot potato. Unfortunately, this repetitive action results in the demise of a relationship. Only by going inside yourself can you name stress, tame it, and transmute it. If you don't regulate the stress that is going on for you, you'll try to control others, especially your partner, and this will negatively impact your relationship.

Knowing how to quiet and calm yourself is vital. No one else can cultivate this skill for you. To begin, you'll need to recognize and identify your stresses.

For directions about how to keep an easy yet eye-opening stress journal, visit my website: **www.lovingforkeeps.com**, then search for "stress journal." You'll be surprised how many times a day you don't feel quite right.

If you don't think you're worthy enough to handle your anxious emotions for your own benefit, then control them for the sake of your loved ones. By not regulating your stress, you will be responsible for damaging those you profess to love the most.

Your myth-busting tour continues. Enjoy the exhilaration, liberation and empowerment of debunking relationship myths.

THE EMOTION MYTH

Feelings are what matter the most in a relationship.

No emotion can take hold of you unless you let it. You have the power to define the emotion; emotions do not define you. You are a person of many states of being, and you can learn how to control these states.

Meditation and other practices can help you attain ephemeral blissful states, but it's crucial that you're able to handle the emotions that flow through you in the moment on a daily basis, not grab on to them or let them grab on to you.

I'm not advocating repression, denial, and sucking it up and stoically moving on. You want emotions to flow through you, process them, let them go, but not dump them on someone else. They are your emotions, no one else's. Furthermore, you don't need to hold on to them to get a sense of your identity. You and every human being are full-spectrum emotional beings, capable of many kinds of feelings.

Story

Over a period of time I was feeling out of sorts when my adult son used to come home for a visit. My husband and my son would be having a great conversation about economics, engineering, or science – topics that I know very little about. I would interject a comment from time and time, but it was obvious that they were annoyed. This kept happening, until I got upset and told them they weren't leaving any room for me to enter into the conversation.

I talked to them about how I felt — alienated, not part of what they were discussing. I wanted them to take care of what I was feeling by getting them to change, and that approach never works.

Later, after my son had left, I came to the conclusion that I was jealous. Then I realized that I didn't want to be jealous of a father and son having their own relationship and conversations that didn't include me. Their relationship is important, and I have my own relationship with my son. I felt relieved after naming the emotion that was plaguing me and ruining my time with my son. Once I got specific and identified the feeling, I could do something about it.

Now when my husband and son are having their conversations, I feel more at ease. I'm not trying to get my two cents in here and there. When I do have something to offer, because I can control my jealousy, my comments are much more appropriate, interesting, and germane to the conversation. By shifting my inner state, I'm able to really enjoy my son's visits and his unique connection to his father, and that's a gift to me and to my son and husband.

❧ ❧ ❧

Busted Myth

If you identify with your feelings, you will not be able to change them. They will control you. You aren't your feelings; you are a human being who has feelings and happens to be feeling a certain way at a certain time. You are a complex human being, not simplistic or static.

Feelings come and go. Let them flow in and out of you. Acknowledge and recognize them, but don't let them take over or define you. Feelings are a state of being, nothing more and nothing less. And, states constantly change. Try to be okay with the changing flow of the full-spectrum person that you are — that everyone is.

If you are attaching too strongly to your feelings, it might be because you're afraid of losing your false identity. Are you overly connected to your feelings because you're afraid that if you got rid of them you might not know who you are?

Fortunately, there is a vast reality that is you. It includes your feelings, but is not strictly limited to them. How about your mind and body? You need to be in touch with your feelings as well as all aspects of who you are in order to be whole and integrated.

Try to become a sleuth about your own behavior and what motivates it. Remember that you always have the power to change what you're feeling if you recognize it and decide you don't like it. Is a particular way that you're feeling causing more harm than good in your life and your relationship? If so, change your thinking, which will change your inner state.

29

Don't ask your partner to manage your state of being for you. Do it yourself. Gain inner strength and personal integrity, which you can then use to enhance and deepen your relationship.

Your myth-busting tour continues. Enjoy the exhilaration, liberation and empowerment of debunking relationship myths.

THE ONENESS MYTH

To have a successful relationship, partners must be on the same path.

A committed relationship is learning how to sail your own boat. Your partner has hers or his and you have yours.

In 2002, when my husband and I were on the verge of divorce, we had to throw away the oneness myth that we were in the same boat. You must destroy this belief, too, if you want your relationship to survive.

If your interpretation of your relationship is that you and your partner are sailing in the same boat, you will eventually feel your relationship is too constrained and suffocating. You'll be in continual combat over which one of you is in charge of the helm. It's a known fact that it's destabilizing to have two captains of a boat. Instead, each partner has to step up to being the captain of her or his own boat.

This is when my students inevitably ask: "Then where is the relationship if we're each sailing separately, charting our own courses?" The answer is: A relationship is the interplay between two interdependent boats.

There are always myriad possibilities that you can choose to experience or not in your relationship, such as: keeping in close

31

contact as you ride out a squall; blowing horns, guiding each other through the fog; anchoring alongside each other to share cocktails, dinner, and sex, while never leaving your boats.

If you leave your boat and join your partner's, you'll find yourself shouting, "Where am I in this relationship?" If you're asking this question, you've jumped ship – which, metaphorically speaking, is yourself. You actually ARE your boat. If you don't know how to captain and live in your own boat, you can't have a deep and meaningful relationship with your partner or with yourself.

Busted Myth

You are not the same as your partner. You have different hopes and dreams. You are two different people even though you're in a relationship that brings you together into an alliance.

You are never on the same path with your partner, or on the same path as anyone else on the planet. You are a unique being. No one has been or ever will be YOU. You and your partner are always sailing in separate boats. If you think you have to be in the same boat, you can never be you to your fullest. You can't be intimate with someone else if you can't understand who you are as a distinct and separate human being.

I'm not dismissing your longings and yearnings for a deep connection with your partner, but becoming one with her or him is not connection — it's an illusion. To demythologize your belief system, you must let go of one of the deadliest myths — that of becoming one with your partner. This is not what you want to aspire to because it's impossible, even though it may feel true in the early stages of a relationship when you and your partner are infatuated with each other.

It's true that you are "one" because you and your partner are human, but you and your partner are always two distinct individuals. It may seem contradictory, but offering yourself as a solid, separate individual to your partner leads to deep love, mind-blowing intimacy, and a delicious sense of unity. On the other hand, seeking "oneness" leads to a sense of being smothered, distant, and losing oneself. So, sail your own boat and be prepared for the most thrilling ride of your life.

Your myth-busting tour continues. Enjoy the exhilaration, liberation and empowerment of debunking relationship myths.

THE IMPORTANCE MYTH

Partners become less important to each other over time.

When you first fall in love, you feel your partner is very important to you. Then time goes by. You face challenges, and disagreements intensify. This may lead you to believe that you and your partner are falling apart, losing importance to each other, but the opposite is true: A long-term partner actually becomes more important, not less.

In fact, if you're in a long-lived relationship, your partner is so important to your life that it's difficult not to feel constrained by her or his opinions, likes, and dislikes.

Here's the challenge: How can you develop your own sense of self in the midst of this growing partner importance? Realizing how important your partner is to you, especially when you're upset with her or him, will turn your thinking downside-up about your relationship issues.

If you feel distant from your partner, it's often because you've become too attached to her or him, and that doesn't feel good. Why? Because when you're overly attached, you don't know who you are, where you begin, and where you end. When the two of you are enmeshed, you can only react, disagree, withdraw, and/or manipulate each other.

Busted Myth

Even if you and your partner aren't spending as much time with each other as you used to or are living parallel lives, you're still triggering each other — and that means you're too close, not distant. You can drive each other crazy only because you both mean a lot to one another, otherwise you'd be indifferent. Emotional heat does not indicate distance.

You become closer to your partner the longer the two of you are together. You become more important to your partner, not less important, even though it might not feel that way. At times you may not love or even like your partner, but you've become very close — in fact, too close for comfort. When you get so attached to, not distant from your partner, you cannot find yourself, because the one you've grown distant from is YOU.

When everything is going great, it makes it even harder to be you because you want your partner to accept you. When you want your partner to approve of you more than you approve of yourself, you know your relationship is in trouble. If your partner is more important to you than you are to yourself, you feel constrained, which is a normal marital dynamic, and you'll have to work harder to expand your sense of self.

Remember, even if you share the same professions and interests, house and bedroom, you are two completely different human beings. Healthy relationships can only be between two complete and whole individuals who retain their separate identities.

Your myth-busting tour continues. Enjoy the exhilaration, liberation and empowerment of debunking relationship myths.

THE SOMETHING FEELS WRONG MYTH

If a relationship is good, then nothing should feel wrong.

When long-term couples are studied cross-culturally — gay, lesbian, and straight —relationships all over the world have the same dynamics. It doesn't matter if couples have lots of sex or little, whether they spend a lot of time with each other or not, etc.

In other words, the bad news is: The places of elation, "stuckness," compromise, constraint, and suffocation are where a long-term relationship takes you. There's no way to avoid these relationship dynamics happening over and over again, in a cyclical fashion.

Even though something feels wrong with your relationship, your relationship is actually all right.

This is how relationship dynamics operate:

Feeling at ease — When you are dating and first fall in love, you are trying to find someone who can make you feel at ease, because being in the world is hard. This new person brings meaning to your life, helps you make sense out of this chaotic world.

Feeling elated — Once you've found that right person, your conversations are about connection, and your fears are minimized. You appreciate your partner and your partner appreciates you. This is the "honeymoon" phase of mutual acceptance and comfort.

Feeling anxious — Stress builds as you start to have arguments. Because you don't know what to do with this anxiety, you blame your partner for it. When you felt fantastic during the "honeymoon" stage, it was because of your partner. Now when you feel lousy, you assume it must be his or her fault.

Feeling compromised — In an attempt to make yourself feel okay, you want to return to the way things used to be between the two of you. So, you try to be acceptable to your partner, but the only way to do so is by compromising yourself. In this process you'll pay the price for sacrificing more and more of who you are, mortgaging your personal integrity by cutting off pieces of yourself. You'll express less and less of the real you — to yourself and to your partner.

Feeling constrained — In this constricted state, you'll ask, "How can I be who I am in my relationship? I can't find myself." Topics of conversation become limited — sex, money, parenting, vacation, in-laws — all of these become hot buttons. Instead of appreciating your partner your partner, you resort to fighting, withdrawing, or both.

Feeling stuck — You can no longer keep adapting to your partner. You feel you have depleted your inner resources. You get stuck and become despairing. When this happens, take heart because it's normal. It might take a few minutes in the heat of an argument, a few days or many decades for this to happen, but this is how relationships unfold. Everything is going right, not wrong.

Feeling squeezed and suffocated — This is the time of going through the eye of the needle. You're not sure you can make it through to the other side to the following:

Freedom and intimacy — You'll never be free unless you can self-reflect and face your inner demons. You can only come through the BIG SQUEEZE by becoming more whole and more full as a person. Even though you have to go through the process on your own — go through the dark nights of the soul — you can do it while still being in your relationship. Your relationship has actually helped propel you to this opportunity for freedom.

All of these phases are in constant flux and are fluid. They can play out before you know it in a marital conversation gone awry, and they are the chronological dynamics in all long-term relationships.

41

Busted Myth

Many couples are disappointed that they can't get to freedom and intimacy, or if they get there, they can't stay there. They erroneously think that if they aren't capable of sustaining a happy union, there's something wrong with their marriage, their partner, or with them. Sometimes they even think they've been mismatched from the very beginning. This usually isn't true. Couples are just naïve and idealistic. They need relationship education to turn their thinking around about real-life marital dynamics.

Conflict, even long-term entrenched conflict, is not necessarily an indication that anything is going wrong — it's simply normal. (Note: I am not talking about physical or sexual abuse.) Sometimes agreeing can be the problem, not disagreeing, because you might have to sacrifice yourself in order to agree. If you feel something isn't "right" in your relationship, think about these bumps as opportunities, signposts for potential personal growth that can lead to a deeper and more satisfying relationship. These so-called obstacles are tailor-made challenges for you to face.

Relationship dynamics are necessary and normal. Since you can't prevent how a relationship evolves anymore than you can the seasons changing or growing older, how you understand and interpret what is going on is the secret key to relationship happiness.

Keep reminding yourself that there's "rightness" to what's happening in your relationship — in every argument you have and in how your relationship evolves — not "wrongness." For most couples this is a huge shift in thinking. How could this information help you transform your relationship?

Your myth-busting tour continues. Enjoy the exhilaration, liberation and empowerment of debunking relationship myths.

THE UNDERSTANDING MYTH

A healthy relationship means that both partners must understand each other.

You will never fully understand your partner, and your partner will never understand you. You can have compassion for each other, but trying to figure out your partner is futile.

Story

On the radio I heard a story about an American artist who lives in Paris and has a studio where he invites tourists from all over the world to come for Sunday dinner. (Visit his website: www.jim-haynes.com. Email jim@jim-haynes.com to reserve your spot, if you're ever in Paris on a Sunday.) Jim and his friends cook up a dinner that people from different countries share. People don't necessarily speak the same language, but they get the chance to come together for a couple of hours and pay just a nominal sum to cover the costs of this feast. When the interviewer commented how these events promoted cross-cultural understanding, Jim Haynes immediately disabused him of this notion. He responded by saying something I've never forgotten — that it's not possible for people to understand each other. There are too many religious, linguistic, and cultural differences. What one American in Paris has been trying to do for over 30 years is help people learn to love each other in spite of what they can't understand.

This is the same story in a long-term relationship.

Busted Myth

Couples waste their time trying to figure out each other; it's just not possible and not necessary in order to love someone. Your partner will never be like you. Stop trying to coerce her or him into thinking like you, into agreeing that you've got the answer about how to live life. You do and your partner does, too. There is room for multiple ways of thinking and being in a couple.

No one ever fully understands why others do the things that they do. You never stop being an individual just because you are in a long-term relationship. Compassion and empathy are possible, but successfully figuring out your partner is not. It's hard enough figuring out what's going on inside of yourself. Love your partner. Forget about trying to understand her or him.

Can you honor and love those you don't understand, especially your partner and yourself?

Your myth-busting tour continues. Enjoy the exhilaration, liberation and empowerment of debunking relationship myths.

THE INEQUALITY MYTH

I can't have a good relationship because my partner is not my equal.

You and your partner have interlocking psychological puzzle pieces. You are different in the ways you each manifest in the world, yet equal. If you weren't equal, you wouldn't be interested in staying with each other.

Fighters and lovers like to team up with those of equal ability. You and your partner are a team of two, of equal abilities, in more ways than you think, even though you may come from very different backgrounds educationally, culturally, and economically.

Story

In my family I was the golden girl, the child who could do no wrong. On the other hand, my husband was the black sheep, the bad boy who could do no right. For decades my husband and I focused on how different our childhood experiences were in our respective families. Now we realize we shared a very similar childhood in this respect: Neither set of parents saw us as three-dimensional human beings. We were boxed into nice little packages marked "good" and "bad."

My husband and I both struggled extra hard with cultivating our sense of self on our own because we were dependent on approval from others. When we were too dependent on others' opinions of us, we gave our power away to someone else to determine how we felt.

This understanding of psychological jigsaw puzzle pieces fitting together has brought us closer together. We no longer fight over our families' and our own "believed" superiority over one another.

How are you and your partner psychological equals?

If this partner equality is true, then who you are is just as valid as who your partner is. What you want and desire is just as important as what your partner wants and desires. No one in a partnership is more or less valuable or inferior or superior to the other. For example, if you don't earn the money to support your family, and your partner is the breadwinner, who you are, how you spend your time, is not less valid. If your partner has a PhD and you only have a GED, you're still equals psychologically, even though there's a disparity in a particular arena of education.

Busted Myth

When my husband is doing activities I don't like, that I can't control, I don't think he is my equal. I often want to denigrate him. If I think he watches too many movies, eats too much, doesn't get enough exercise, I think he is beneath me in what he values and how he decides to spend his time. Where does that thinking lead me except to a place of judgment?

The better question to ask myself on a continual basis is: Why would I want to be with someone who isn't my equal? People don't stay friends or lovers with those who aren't their equal. That can be a sobering realization, especially if you don't like whom you're hanging around with.

Your partner, if you've been with her or him for a long time, complements you perfectly. The old adage that opposites attract may be true, but on the inside you and your partner have similar psychologies. Your partner is a great mirror for you. So, if you don't like whom you're looking at, change yourself — and that will help your partner change, as well.

A healthy relationship is not about one person losing and the other one winning, jockeying for a superior position over one another. It's about knowing that both you and your partner are of equal worth and can increase in value together.

Your myth-busting tour continues. Enjoy the exhilaration, liberation and empowerment of debunking relationship myths.

REPLACEMENT MYTH

I'd be much happier if I replaced the long-term partner that I have now with someone else.

Long-lived couples are perfect psychological matches, which means that the two parts of a duo are irreplaceable. Every human being is completely unique. Your partner is not a swappable part. There'll never be a person just like you or your partner, and there never was one exactly like either of you in the past. You can always choose to be with another partner, but that only changes one part of the equation — your partner, not you.

If you resonate with this myth, perhaps this exercise will disabuse you of believing that substituting your partner for someone else is what you need to do in order to be happy.

Exercise

Make a list of the similarities and differences of your partner and you.

Take a piece of paper and draw a line down the middle of the page. At the top of one column, write your name. At the top of the other column, write your partner's name.

You could start off with physical characteristics, just to get the flow going. For example, in my column I'd write "petite and thin." In my husband's, I'd write "tall and robust." Next I might write in my column, "loves opera." In my husband's I might write, "loves opera." Proceed in this fashion.

After you do this exercise for a few minutes, look over your two-column list. Maybe you'll end up seeing more similarities than differences —in all realms. Most couples focus too much on their differences, not their commonalities, and on how they don't get along.

(If you don't have a partner right now, do this exercise about a previous relationship.)

Review what you've written.

Can you see how some of these differences and similarities exquisitely interlock? Does it make sense that you are with the partner you are with?

Busted Myth

The replacement theory doesn't work because humans aren't machines. Maybe this question would be more apropos as follows: "If I've made no efforts to change myself, how can I have a flourishing new relationship with someone else?"

Since every human being is unique and special, no one is replaceable. You may think that you can get rid of your long-term partner and get together with someone else and everything will be fine, but life doesn't usually work that way. You're still the other half of a couple, and you'll continue with the same behaviors unless you've done the inner work to understand yourself in new ways.

Instead of saying your partner needs replacing, maybe you're the one who needs to be replaced, and you can only do that by changing yourself. If you've gone through a personal transformation and your present relationship continues to be unsatisfying, creating happiness in your next relationship will be more possible

Too many divorces happen without either partner making personal changes that will help them succeed later on in a new relationship. That's why the statistics for divorced people building new, fulfilling relationships are so grim.

The cards are stacked against you if you refuse to change yourself. And if you decide to change yourself you may just find, as my husband and I did, that your existing partner is exactly the person you want.

Your myth-busting tour continues. Enjoy the exhilaration, liberation and empowerment of debunking relationship myths.

THE VICTIM MYTH

If I am wounded in a relationship, I am a victim.

Busting this myth is politically incorrect. Most people can't stop themselves from revisiting their relationship wounds over and over again, and people seem to relish wallowing in self-pity.

I'm very respectful of every human's narrative, the story of their life and what's happened to them, but I'm more dedicated to personal growth and transformation. It's straightforward: You won't be able to move forward in your life if you want to keep believing in woundology and your victimhood.

If you were physically, sexually, or emotionally abused as a child, you were a victim. There was nothing you could do about it. As an adult, if you are abused in any way by your partner or anyone else you are in a relationship with, you do have options, if you're willing to exercise them.

If you are not able to take full responsibility for who you are and want to become and can't get beyond blaming your parents, your partner, your circumstances, your education, etc., your life is not your own and you will not be able to grow up.

Busted Myth

People who play the victim don't have to be responsible for their lives. They feel justified holding steadfast to their tragic story. You're not responsible for what happens to you, but you are responsible for how you respond to it and handle it. How can you learn from every experience that you have — the good, the bad, and the ugly? Negative experiences cannot be denied, but they must be reframed in order for you to lead a fulfilling life.

Responsible adults are not abandoned or victims in relationships, only children are. You can be left by your partner, not abandoned by her or him. You always have alternative paths to follow. If you can't see them, then you might need professional help to transform your perception, or to help you leave an abusive situation you are enduring. The words "abandoned "and "victim" are so loaded that they render you powerless. Get them out of your vocabulary so that you can grow up to be an emotionally mature adult.

Please forgive the oversimplification of a highly controversial topic that could be debated for hours on end and about which countless books have been researched and written; but I implore you to embrace a new perspective. You will see huge changes in your life, no matter what has happened to you in the past.

Everyone has had some kind of trauma happen to them, even if you can't name or consciously remember it. Whenever you feel disempowered, you are tapping into being a victim. Be vigilant and say NO to the seduction of your wounds, the worst part of a human experience instead of what's the best part, your resilience and strength.

Beyond physical or sexual abuse, which should not be tolerated in any form, we all feel at one point or another victimized by our partner. If you choose to remain the "victim," nothing will ever change. Once you stop identifying yourself as a victim in your relationship, however, you will realize you have the power of choice. You can use that strength to change your relationship for the better.

Your myth-busting tour continues. Enjoy the exhilaration, liberation and empowerment of debunking relationship myths.

THE HATE MYTH

Partners in a healthy relationship never hate each other.

It's only natural that you might not want to admit that you have vindictive feelings toward your partner, the one you're supposed to love the most, but you do. It's not pathological. It's normal because love and hate are flipsides of the same coin.

"Schadenfreude," a term that means that pleasure is derived from the misfortunes of others, plays out when you're jealous and envious. Can you honestly say that you have never been guilty of entertaining these feelings of being upset because someone has what you'd like to have? You don't always want the best for others (unless you can have it, too) and that sometimes includes your partner.

This realization can be excruciatingly painful, but it's part of what manifests in the lives of every couple, bar none. You might find it hard to accept the totality — the light and dark sides — of who you are. You'd probably rather cherry pick the acceptable parts of yourself, but that will leave you feeling fake and un-integrated.

Recognizing and acknowledging hatred for what it actually is help you stop the cycle of denial about who you are. You aren't a bad person for feeling hate toward your partner. If you keep denying an emotion, it can't give you any information.

When you hate your partner, what is the information you're getting about who you are?

The answer to this question is vital for your personal development. Hatred isn't your dark side, but denying its existence might be.

Busted Myth

It is essential to be able to reconcile this paradoxical tension of simultaneously hating and loving your partner. People who can't acknowledge that they feel hate are often the ones who perpetuate it the most, unconscious of their destructive behavior. Managing an emotion isn't possible if there's no admission that it even exists. If you have ever said to your partner that you'd never do anything to hurt her or him, you've told one big fat lie.

Love and hate are both part of a relationship. You can't have one without the other. The light and dark side make a relationship whole. You have to learn to reconcile these two strong emotions. It is completely normal and non-pathological to feel occasional hate for someone you love. What this strong emotion directed toward someone else says about you is what you need to look at.

Some of my students take issue with the word "hate." They think it's too harsh and intense. They ask these questions: "Is hate momentary or long-lasting? Maybe I've acted from the worst part of who I am toward my partner? Is that hate?"

If you don't want to use the word "hate," then don't get hung up on semantics and substitute it with "dislike" or any other word you'd prefer. The important thing is to be open to seeing how this paradox operates in your relationship and not deny that it does. When you see it clearly, you can then deal with what it is in you that causes this "unacceptable" emotion. And that new realization can actually lead you to a healthier sense of self and a more open and rewarding relationship.

Your myth-busting tour continues. Enjoy the exhilaration, liberation and empowerment of debunking relationship myths.

THE LOVE MYTH

The heart of all successful relationships is unconditional love.

Love is conditional. Unconditional love does not exist.

Loving your partner makes you emotionally vulnerable. Because you are vulnerable, you and your partner have the power to repeatedly hurt each other.

Most of us have been guilty of at least some of these less-than-virtuous acts in our long-term relationships:

1. Maybe you've committed acts of tardiness. What does it mean to leave your partner waiting for you, time after time? If you believe in the Golden Rule — "Do unto others as you would have them do unto you"— could you really call your disregard for punctuality "love"?

2. In the sexual realm, do you fake orgasms or tell your partner that you don't have them when you do?

Partners often emotionally torment each other while pretending that they don't.

It's hard being loving when you're unhappy in your relationship, but when everything is going well, you're still deluded if you think that everything you do is in the name of love.

You might withhold love because that's what you learned how to do to survive your childhood. Every family withholds love in one way or another. "If you do this, I'll love you; and if you don't, I won't." You got more love when you did this and less when you did that. Have you ever been accepted or loved unconditionally?

Busted Myth

How can unconditional love exist when it doesn't exist for yourself? Love for yourself is conditional. At times I love myself more than at other times. Don't you? And, it's usually because of something I did or didn't do, or thought about or didn't think about. You do the same to your partner, and she or he to you.

Love is a powerful emotion that is hard to tolerate. Maybe you can give it, but can you receive it? Since unconditional love doesn't exist, you can't ask for the same kind of love from your partner that you might fantasize you had from your parents. Your partner is not your mother or your father. And, if you contemplate the love even your parents felt for you, wasn't it often really conditional? You knew what pleased and displeased them, didn't you? The only person you need to learn how to love and accept unconditionally is YOU.

❧ ❧ ❧

Monogamy puts you in a pressure cooker. It forces you to either blame and be mean to your partner, or to dig deep within yourself and find new growth. Love is the answer, and it does triumph the more you are able to love yourself. You cannot give to your partner what you do not have.

Your myth-busting tour continues. Enjoy the exhilaration, liberation and empowerment of debunking relationship myths.

THE SELF CARE MYTH

My partner should take care of me.

Everyone is codependent on some level, and that's why it's important to recognize and be vigilant of your codependent tendencies. My definition of codependence is — any time when you're not taking care of yourself. And, I'm not talking about narcissism.

Taking care of yourself is your number-one priority. Your partner wasn't born to take care of you. You were born to take care of yourself.

You aren't taking care of yourself if you're overwhelmed, fearful, depressed, over-reacting, spending most of your time caregiving, needing others to make you feel okay, living a life of shoulds and have-tos, having to have everything perfect, not being able to make decisions, and so forth. This list of addictive qualities could go on and on. Yes, these qualities — some of them wonderful, such as being generous and caring — are addictive, if you can't choose NOT to do them.

As an adult, you are responsible for your wellbeing in all realms — physical, emotional, intellectual, and financial — which doesn't mean you have to be the money earner in your partnership, but you do have to know how to manage your finances. You need to solve your own issues, meet your own needs, and heal your own wounds. This is not narcissism; it's not being selfish; it's being self-full, filling yourself up.

Busted Myth

Taking care of yourself is about being healthy and balanced, and it's the most important part of a relationship. It might feel uncomfortable at first to take care of yourself, but you are automatically worthy of it. Everyone is. Yes, your partner might take care of you when you're ill, but she or he needs to take care of her or his own life, as well. If you're only devoted to the well-being of your partner and not to your own, you're codependent.

An adult takes 100 percent responsibility for his or her actions, emotions, and thoughts. Why is taking care of yourself so important? Because if you don't, you'll want to control your partner to get what you want. You'll want to impose your will on others, especially your partner, to get your needs met, your problems solved. Operating in the world from a place of inner "fullness" instead of inner "emptiness" feels very different and has world-apart different results.

Don't fool yourself; there are false ways of taking care of yourself. Taking care of yourself at the expense of others isn't acceptable.

Here are a couple of examples:

If you go shopping and buy something for yourself, spending more than you can afford and overextending your credit, you are not taking care of yourself, even though you may have participated in some momentary retail therapy. When you can't pay your charge card, the consequences for you or your family are ultimately not positive.

You are not taking care of yourself by raging and yelling at your partner, even though it might make you feel better to vent. If you have to wreak havoc and demean others to feel better, you are not taking care of yourself — or anybody else around you.

How have you fooled yourself into thinking that you're taking care of yourself? Getting drunk? Watching 12-hours of an HBO series all at once? You don't have to be a goody two shoes, but you do have to be the judge of whether you're using your time wisely or not.

The rewards of managing your own self are many. You become more solid. You feel better about your place in the world. And you can offer your partner deep and real love that doesn't ask her or him to do something for you in return. Believe me, when you experience this kind of love, it will really rock your world.

Codependents Anonymous (www.coda.org) is a helpful organization whose mandate is to promote healthy relationships with oneself and others. If you go on their website, you'll find meeting times — all over the USA and abroad. Meetings are free. They also have some substantive handouts that will help you understand how ubiquitous codependent behavior really is.

Your myth-busting tour continues. Enjoy the exhilaration, liberation and empowerment of debunking relationship myths.

THE PARTNER MYTH

My partner makes me feel bad.

How do you kick the habit of trying to fix your partner instead of yourself?

Since control of others or situations is an illusion, the only one you can transform is yourself. Then, why spend more time trying to change your partner instead of yourself? If you think that if your partner were different, you'd be happy, it's not true. You'd be happier if you'd change.

If you don't master your thoughts and emotions, you can't get close to anyone. You can't enjoy the fruits of life or love.

Busted Myth

Stop focusing on everyone else. Focus on YOU. If you're blaming your partner for what's going wrong in your life, you're not focusing on you. Know what you can change and what you can't. You can't change your partner's problems. Your partner's problems are hers or his — not yours. You can be detached from your partner's issues and still be very caring. If you're too attached to your partner's well-being, then your partner has the power to determine whether you're happy or sad — not you. No matter how hard you try, you can't be the emotional savior of anyone but yourself.

In a healthy relationship, there's no one to blame or shame, and nothing to justify or defend. Your partner can't make you feel what you don't already feel. You might not be conscious of what your feelings about yourself are. So, when your partner triggers a particular feeling, she or he can only do that because you already have that feeling inside you. Feelings of unworthiness, low self-esteem, etc. are deep seated. When your partner criticizes you, you get upset because you already are your own harshest critic about the very behavior that your partner points out to you.

A vibrant relationship flourishes because of you. Put the attention on you. What can you change within yourself? Only you can nourish yourself. A blossoming YOU creates a blossoming relationship.

Your myth-busting tour continues. Enjoy the exhilaration, liberation and empowerment of debunking relationship myths.

THE SEX MYTH

My sexual prime was when I was young.

Sex has evolved, and it gets better the older you get.

A half-million years ago a few changes took place which made human sexuality more complex, amazing, and problematic. Women started to have monthly menstrual cycles. They wanted to have sex for the pleasure of it, not just to conceive. Couples stayed together in monogamous partnerships for periods of time. Face-to-face intercourse became possible. Couples could look into each other's eyes and commune while they copulated.

With this transition from purely biologically and hormonally driven sex came desire for a specific partner. And this is when sexual desire became inhibited. The neocortex developed, and this evolution of the brain gave humans the capacity to integrate love, passion, intimacy, beauty, fun, and meaning into sexuality.

Sex has no inherent meaning unless you add it. The only way you can do that is by becoming who you are. That's why older couples have the possibility of having more meaningful sex than their younger counterparts, but only if they're willing to age gracefully and integrate their cellulite and beer bellies into their sex life.

It's difficult to reach your sexual potential, because as you age you might hold back from sexual expression because you are seduced by the media hype about tight derrieres and perky breasts. You might worry about your unsightly stretch marks, your flaccid penis, or your bulging varicose veins. You might idealize taut, hydrated skin, and fall into falsely thinking that the younger people are having all the fun.

You've just fallen for the multi-million-dollar ad campaigns. The good news is: Sex is richer and has a broader range of meanings as you age, not fewer.

Busted Myth

Contrary to popular belief, your genitals are not your major sex organs — your brain and your heart are. Passion goes beyond biological urges and sexual arousal. People don't make love with their penis and vagina. Your imaginative mind plays the key role in sex.

Genital and sexual primes are different. It takes a lifetime to understand who you are sexually.

Why do we keep worshipping young, inexperienced lovers who only have their physical beauty to bring to a sexual encounter? Young people don't understand themselves in ways that older people do. They haven't done the same amount of inner exploration. Sex is better with sagging and wrinkled bodies because you bring a more robust and fully developed self to share. Your "self" development is the heart of your sexual prime, which can keep getting better. If you haven't experienced that to be true, then you haven't grown up yet.

Sexual satisfaction isn't measured by bigger and better orgasms. Orgasms are not the only goal of a great sex life. What we humans are yearning for when we have sex are the strong, transcendent emotions of love and joy that make time "stop"— make us hear "music," make us cry, and laugh. We want to be moved — deeply cared for, and seen as beautiful beings.

No matter how you look as you age, exploring your eroticism — which is essentially your sexual creativity — with your mind, body, and soul is the goal. Your genitals are still part of the package, but you're old enough now to integrate the fullness of who you are, not just settle for the sexual function of your vulva or your penis. You've grown old enough to integrate the whole shebang until you die of old age.

Despite what the advertising industry wants to tell you, your most mind-blowing sexual experiences lie ahead of you, not behind. Bring your full self to your next erotic encounter with your partner and you will be wowed.

Your myth-busting tour continues. Enjoy the exhilaration, liberation and empowerment of debunking relationship myths.

THE DESIRE MYTH

My partner and I should have equal sexual desire for each other because that means we are compatible.

How about the inequality of desire? One partner wants sex when the other one doesn't.

As in anything — going dancing, cleaning the house, going on a date, cooking, etc. — there is always a higher and a lower desire partner. One partner says YES and the other says NO.

When it comes to sex, the YES and NO positions have their pros and cons. The good news is: There's supposed to be a higher and lower desire partner in every twosome. That's how the marriage system works. This push and pull can drive you crazy OR help you have a deeply satisfying sex life.

This is liberating information: The low desire or high desire partner is not gender specific. Men are not always the high desire partners. Women want sex just as much as men do. In every couple, even in same sex ones, there's a high and low desire position. The level of sexual desire is also relative, meaning that you could be high in one relationship and low in another. So, there's no need to identify yourself as a cold fish or a sex fiend; it all depends on who you are and whom you're with.

Couples get divorced over sexual desire tension. I almost did. Once my husband and I understood desire dynamics, we stopped quarreling over each other's demands and expectations.

Busted Myth

You and your partner don't have equal sexual desire for each other because you are two separate beings. You don't have identical desire about doing anything in your life. So, why would sex be different?

Every couple has a high and low sexual desire partner. This is how a long-term relationship system plays out. Neither position feels great, but that's the reality. Instead of demanding each other be the same, ask yourself the following questions: Do you want to have sex out of a fullness of who you are or because you're lacking and you want your partner to fill you up?

Do you have sex to manipulate your partner, or maybe to calm down your anxieties, not because you want your partner? Wanting your partner more than he or she wants you is at the heart of the sexual power struggle. Are you more concerned with your partner wanting you than you wanting your partner? Not wanting to desire your partner is an attempt to self-protect against the pain of rejection.

Exercise

Identify yourself as the low or high desire partner in your present relationship. (You might have been just the opposite in a previous relationship, because desire is always a relative position.)

Make a list of the pros and cons of your position.

Here are the two questions for the Quick-Write:
(For directions on how to do a Quick-Write, visit my website: **www.lovingforkeeps.com**, then search for "quick-write.")
How does it feel to have low desire?
Or…How does it feel to have high desire?

Share your comments with your partner. This exercise helps you realize that the low and the high desire partner both suffer. Neither position is ideal. Sometimes high and low desire partners express themselves in similar ways. Maybe the entrenched position you've been holding isn't really what you want. Polarization can be damaging to you and/or to your partner.

Can you have more compassion for each other once you understand that desire inequality is normal? Not coercing your partner into having the same amount of sexual desire as you allows more room for juicy sex to actually take place.

Your myth-busting tour continues. Enjoy the exhilaration, liberation and empowerment of debunking relationship myths.

79

THE ADORATION MYTH

My partner should adore me.

A single friend of mine, who has never been married, once told me he thought a woman should love him more than he should love her. I told him that he was really talking about adoration, not love. This is the way he distanced himself from all the women in his life, and the way he protected himself from being vulnerable.

If you want to be adored and worshiped, you'll never be able to sustain a deep, satisfying, and challenging long-term relationship.

Beautiful and successful people often fall prey to adoration instead of the real thing — love. They think that a partner fawning all over them is fulfilling, but it never is.

No matter who you are, you probably fantasize about this kind of adoring love, even though it is shallow and superficial. You might get seduced because adoration is not vulnerable while love is. Being vulnerable means you're open and susceptible to emotional pain. But, you can't safeguard yourself from suffering unless you never want to give and receive love.

When you express what you want to your partner, you're exposed, dangling out on a limb. This vulnerable position doesn't feel that great, but it's the only way to have a life worth living.

Busted Myth

Often people who want to be adored have big egos and personas, but very little self-esteem substance because they don't know who they are. They define themselves by what others think of them and cannot stand up on their own without an adoring audience. They don't understand that approving of themselves is no one else's business but theirs.

Don't you want your partner to love you and for you to love her or him? Adoration is not the same as love. Worshiping someone, idolizing someone, is not deep and real. Don't settle for someone who makes you feel adored. It's compelling, I know, but it's an illusion.

You can't know who you are if you're always dependent on your partner's high opinion of you. What counts is what you think of yourself — not egotistically, but in a centered manner. It's the only way you can be intimate with yourself, which is the first step to being intimate with your partner.

Partners who want to sit back, do nothing, and be adored cannot tolerate the vulnerability involved in monogamy. They often want an entourage of people or lovers constantly propping them up and telling them how wonderful they are. Or, they'll play victim and never take responsibility for any conflict, claiming that it's always someone else's fault.

To love and honor yourself, you need to have a sense of who you are. How you get a greater sense of self is by answering life's big questions, such as —

How To Save Your Relationship...From Yourself

1. Do you know what you're worth, and I don't mean monetarily? If you don't find value in yourself, how can you find value in your partner?

2. Are you a prisoner of what your partner thinks of you? If you take everything personally and are so attached to what your partner thinks about you, you can't know how you feel about yourself.

Adoring your partner or having your partner adore you may appeal to your fairytale notions of knights and princesses, but these archetypes aren't real people.

Get real. Love is infinitely superior to adoration, even though it hurts. You can't have the highs in life without the lows.

Your myth-busting tour continues. Enjoy the exhilaration, liberation and empowerment of debunking relationship myths.

THE FOREVER MYTH

My relationship with my partner will last forever, especially if I do the work I need to do.

It takes a lot of courage to be in a long-term relationship. You don't have any control over when it will end, and it will eventually break up one way or another — your partner will leave you or you'll leave him or her.

The only thing you do know for sure in a relationship is this: Your partner will leave you by his or her own volition by walking out or by dying. That is the only guarantee in a relationship, but it's not the guarantee you want. It is, however, all you get — unless, of course, you walk out or die first.

How can you open yourself up when you know that there's only loss on the other side? Yet, you do this all the time, consciously and unconsciously — living life knowing that you'll die.

Busted Myth

We never want things to change, yet that's all life is — change. We also believe in cause and effect. For example, if we do everything "right" for ourselves and for our relationship, everything will work out and be just what we envisioned.

Unfortunately, that's not how real life always plays out, no matter how hard we try.

As in life, in a relationship there are no guarantees. You'll desperately want them, but they aren't possible. Inherent in relationships is loss. You never know when your partner will leave you — either by choice or by death. Or, you might be the one to leave. You can say that'll never happen, but this would be imprudent. What if your partner suddenly started behaving in harmful ways? You might have to leave to save yourself. Change is loss; loss is change. Never say never.

One of the biggest challenges is living the paradox — loving with all your might while knowing that loss is always lurking in the background. When you embrace love, loss comes with it; they walk hand-in-hand, one intensifying the other.

Your myth-busting tour continues. Enjoy the exhilaration, liberation and empowerment of debunking relationship myths.

THE HONEYMOON MYTH

My honeymoon was the pinnacle of my marriage.

When you want to get back to the honeymoon phase in your relationship, what are you referring to? Infatuation with minimal conflict, mutual admiration — and hot, or at least frequent, sex?

The euphoria of the honeymoon isn't supposed to last. It's not possible to retrieve it from your past and relive it. Actually, it's not worthwhile trying, because whether you had a great honeymoon stage or a mediocre one, what's ahead of you is better than you ever dreamed of, even though you'll have to go through the experiences of humdrum sex and mean-spirited fights with your partner to get there.

Confusion and pain are ultimately purposeful, and it's important to view them in this vein. Marital experiences are not gratuitous; they will eventually lead you to hidden treasure. You won't be able to open the treasure chests, however, unless you discover where the keys are hidden. Busting each relationship myth, especially this one about the honeymoon, gives you another possibility to share in the myriad riches of a long-term relationship.

Busted Myth

Your long-term relationship wants to grow forward. To keep thinking that the early stages were the only worthwhile times denigrates you and your partner.

Wishing that your relationship were still like your "honeymoon" is unrealistic and counterproductive. Youth-oriented culture and media perpetuate this myth. Without the honeymoon phase, couples might not commit for the long-term. But if your relationship stayed at the honeymoon level, it would mean that you're not growing and developing. The honeymoon is intense, immature love, no matter what age you fall in love. A long-term relationship is about the deep satisfactions of becoming an adult.

My wedding day was one of the best days of my life, but it's such a small part of what my husband and I have created together over the last 35 years. It's a lovely memory that pales in comparison to what we feel for each other now.

How can you move your relationship from honeymoon adolescence to maturity?

1. Stop proving anything to your partner. Do what you love to do, what excites you. Your partner will be turned on and energized by what fulfills you — because there'll be more and more of who you are to love.

2. Manage your fears in order to dare to come up with creative ideas for fun activities and adventures to do together in the world and in your bedroom.

If you feel the vibe is gone in your relationship, it can be resuscitated if you stop holding on to the past and let your relationship grow forward.

By busting through myths like this honeymoon one, you will be one of the lucky few that has the chance for an extraordinary relationship. It's cause for celebration that relationships can get better and better, and not worse and worse, as you've been led to believe. Go for the gusto of ripening love.

Your myth-busting tour continues. Enjoy the exhilaration, liberation and empowerment of debunking relationship myths.

THE INTIMACY MYTH

Intimacy in a relationship requires mutual trust, acceptance, and baring your souls.

The meaning of intimacy begs to be redefined. Couples are yearning for something that they can't get, because they don't know what it is.

Humans are capable of something very unique — sophisticated language and self-reflection. It takes a neocortex to do this, and a neocortex is what humans have. We're lucky to be able to be intimate, but what does this mean?

Intimacy is not about unconditional love. It's not about being understood, emotionally supported, or getting what you want from your partner to validate and affirm you. It's not about becoming one with your partner. It's not about communicating, negotiating, or doing any kind of technique exceptionally well.

Then what is it? To be capable of being intimate means that first you have to know who you are as a person apart from your partner. And second, you share that self with your partner. The dictionary definition of intimacy is — sharing what is innermost about YOU. If love is about generosity, then you've got to have a YOU to share. Intimacy flourishes because you have a profound relationship with yourself and you are capable of sharing that robust self at its deepest, most vulnerable levels with your partner.

Intimacy with your partner, however, doesn't have a linear trajectory. It develops through conflict and challenges. After going through tough times together, you become capable of revealing who you are in front of your partner, and taking the risk that your partner will still love and want you.

Busted Myth

Intimacy, when it is felt by both partners simultaneously, is amazing. And intimacy experienced only by you and not your partner is equally amazing. Intimacy is analogous to an individual or mutual orgasm. If you don't both climax together, sex has still been worth it, right?

Intimacy does not necessarily reveal itself like a Hallmark moment. Intimacy comes about through the courage to expose who you are to your partner without any guarantees of any reciprocity. Your partner might not reveal anything about her or himself, but you have to. Standing unprotected, emotionally naked in front of the person who is the most important in your life, you are offering your partner who you really are. This step into intimacy may not result in a comfy, cozy feeling, but it is a moment of truth and is deeply moving.

How can a new way of thinking about intimacy be empowering?

Story

The other night my husband and I were gazing into each other's eyes. I felt such tenderness toward my husband. I could see him when he was young. Then he morphed into an old man. Then I saw his death mask. I felt close to tears. This was an intimate moment for me while it wasn't for my husband. In the past, I would have been upset about him not experiencing what I did at the same level of intensity. When we feel that intimacy together, it's wonderful, but not mandatory. I could tell my husband about my experience and accept that he didn't feel the same way.

Visit my website **www.lovingforkeeps.com** for two potent exercises that will help you create intimacy. One is on hugging and the other is on eye-gazing. (Use the website's "search bar" to find these blogs.)

Letting yourself be known and be seen can feel liberating, even if your partner has a negative reaction to your self-revelation. Once you feel these heroic and exhilarating emotions, you'll want to savor more intimate moments, even though they are ephemeral. And when you couple these deep, intimate moments with sex, watch out! It will turn your world inside out with its intensity.

Your myth-busting tour continues. Enjoy the exhilaration, liberation and empowerment of debunking relationship myths.

THE COMMUNICATION MYTH

If my partner and I could learn communication techniques, we would have a perfect relationship.

Most relationship books and therapies concentrate on improving communication skills as a way to enhance connection. Couples learn endless dos and don'ts that are all forgotten in the heat of an argumentative moment because they are pasted-on techniques.

I don't teach techniques. You'll figure out what works for you and what doesn't after you rewire your understanding about relationship topics. If you don't believe in what you're doing, relationship techniques won't work. Or, they might work for a short while, but fail over the long haul.

Busted Myth

You and your partner are always communicating very well, verbally and non-verbally. Most of the time, you just don't want to hear what your partner is relating to you.

If what your partner says is right, it might be too painful to accept. You might have to make a change in your behavior, and that's hard. A lot of what you and your partner have to say to each other is spot-on. The two of you know each other well.

Often the way a communication is expressed obfuscates the nugget of important information. Be curious about what your partner has to say, even if it pushes your buttons.

Story

How often have you had a conversation with your partner that is completely honest? What if you could have the same interaction on three different levels in order to uncover the essence of your relationship and go from that "stuckness" to a place of intimacy? With one banal conversation that my husband and I had, this is exactly what we did.

Here's the transcript of the first of three conversations that my husband and I had.

> *"Hey, I bought a CD from a cute girl when I was in town. She was really pretty. She was selling her CDs at a booth in front of Pete's Café," he said.*
>
> *"Was it sexy?" I asked.*
>
> *"Why did you ask that?" he replied.*
>
> *"I thought you were going to tell me that there was something surprising or weird about the CD. How do you know she's really a singer, or what?" I explained.*
>
> *"I haven't even played it yet. You never listen. There you go, assuming and jumping to conclusions. I hate that about you," he exclaimed.*

For the previous few weeks, our relationship was sweet, even-keeled, and sexually exciting at times. Even though we were under some stress because of my husband's work and a family graduation, we'd spent time with each other and were enjoying life. Did this charged conversation come about due to overload and tiredness after a big graduation weekend? Maybe we should just forget it happened, but we couldn't.

By evening there was a distance between us, even though we had dinner and took a walk together. Something was off between us, and it was palpable. What were we trying to say to each other? How could we resolve the uneasy, messy feelings?

We didn't realize that our disagreement wasn't about the content of what was said —disagreements hardly ever are. We had to study the meta language, what was underneath our words.

(Reconstructing and dissecting the surface level of the he said/she said of an argument is never worthwhile if you want to find out more about who you are. In your desire to be right, to justify your position, you destroy your relationship, not nurture it.)

Here's the transcript of the second conversation on the same topic that my husband and I had.

> *"Hey, I bought a CD from a cute girl this morning because I feel pretty horny and you haven't been too interested in sex while you've been running around making all the plans for the graduation. I'm a bit depressed about my job situation, which is turning out to be not what I expected it to be," he stated.*
>
> *"Yeah, I haven't been interested in sex because there's been too much to do. I'm trying to unwind in my own way. I didn't mean to demean you because you paid attention to a beautiful woman*

in the street. I've bought stuff from cute guys before, too. I'm just feeling worn down right now," I replied.

Several days later we replayed our parts. In the second version of the same conversation, we were more courageous in the moment, each one of us understanding the role we were playing.

We took the risk to stand up to ourselves, not against each other, and be honest about our feelings. We were a little less anxious and a little less reactive. We were trying to study what happened in our interactions and become detectives figuring out what was going on, because our relationship was pretty stable before we had this embarrassing blowout.

Here's the transcript of the third conversation on the same topic that my husband and I had.

> *"I'm feeling lousy about who I am right now. I want you to make me feel better. I know you can't do that. I'm resisting taking responsibility for my life right now. I want to have sex with you because I love you, not just because I feel needy and empty and I expect you to make me feel good. That way it would be a gift, not a repair," he said.*
>
> *"I'm sick of repressing my sexual desires, thinking that they aren't an integral part of the wholeness of who I am. I want you, but I'm not always sure I want myself. I'd like to take the sexual initiative more, but I'm scared that you'll reject me. Why do I want everything else to be perfect—the house, the plans—before I feel I can take the time to sexually play? These things will never be in perfect order. You are the most important person in the world to me and even though that sometimes terrifies me, I'm*

*certainly not showing you how much you mean to me by my
actions," I said.*

When we got to the essence behind the words and the feelings in
our third attempt, this mundane conversation became something
else altogether.

This is how any interchange can be understood on three levels,
each one expressing a deeper meaning, ultimately leading to an
intimate moment. In this instance, intimacy happened only after
we faced ourselves, found some meaning in the pain we were
each going through, and started to accept, love, and have
compassion for ourselves. We were no longer judging and asking
for approval from each other. We took a risk by talking about
our fears, taking responsibility, and feeling remorse for our
actions and non-actions. This leap was taken with absolutely no
guarantees about how these self-revelations were going to be
received. All of this could have ended in humiliation or rejection.

※ ※ ※

Since we've been a couple for decades, why do we ever have
Conversation 1? Because we're human and perfectly fallible, no
matter how much experience we have being married. We forget
that we can only get a feeling of being valued in our marriage if
we claim it for ourselves. We are sometimes still afraid to take full
responsibility for who we are, then end up blaming each other.

Conversations 1, 2 and 3 took place over several days, not within
the time it has taken you to read this. But, when my husband and
I made the bold move to Conversation 3, we were heroic. We got
to feel inner strength that we hardly knew we had.

We're in our early 60s now, continually striving for an extraordinary marriage filled with intimate moments. And, when we leap from the normal to the extraordinary, the fairytale ideal of marriage fades in comparison to the depth and richness of reality.

Your myth-busting tour continues. Enjoy the exhilaration, liberation and empowerment of debunking relationship myths.

THE COMPROMISE MYTH

I can have a great relationship if I negotiate, compromise, and make pacts and agreements with my partner.

Compromising who you are in order to stay with your partner is not necessary. In fact, it's contraindicated. Settling issues by concessions and making pacts with each other don't work in the long run.

If you cut parts off of who you are and sacrifice your sense of self, you'll be resentful that you're no longer a whole and complete person — and you'll blame your partner for diminishing you.

If you're feeling constrained in your relationship because you've compromised yourself, you don't have to run away; but you will have to change your belief system. Successful marriages do not require compromises that demand you give up who you are.

Busted Myth

You'll have a great relationship if you don't do any of the above. The only thing that's required of you to do with your partner is to be you to the fullest you can be. Even if you and your partner disagree in many arenas, you can always make the alliance with each other to respect your differing opinions. Neither one of you needs to convince the other that she or he is right.

In every healthy relationship, there's always room for two complete individuals to manifest who they are and maintain the integrity of their own identities and their own values.

Negotiations, compromises, pacts, and agreements with your partner are short-term band-aids, doomed to fail because they are superficial remedies. A long-term relationship is not a business. Relationships work when each partner has been willing to confront her or himself, not sacrifice or mortgage personal integrity in order to stay together. If a relationship with your partner is worth more than the relationship with yourself and you have to adapt too much to your partner, your relationship cannot develop to its full fruition and will ultimately become unsatisfying.

Everything you decide to do comes with a price. Self-sacrifice isn't worth paying in a relationship. Yes, there's sacrifice when you're raising children, when your partner is ill, when death visits your family, and other extenuating circumstances, but if you think compromise is the glue that's keeping you and your partner together, it actually is undermining what you are trying to preserve.

Some of my students have made extensive signed agreements with their partners that they end up feeling guilty about breaking. If you want to make pacts with anyone, make them with yourself and then have the integrity to keep them.

Story

My husband is a great ballroom dancer, but he doesn't enjoy it as much as I do. Recently, he decided that he doesn't like dancing that much anymore while I still love it. We didn't compromise. We didn't make any kind of tit-for-tat agreement — if you go dancing, I'll do this or that. Of course, I'm disappointed that my husband made this decision about something that is fun to share together, but what can I realistically do about it other than get angry and resentful? Note that my husband didn't tell me he never wanted to go dancing again — he said that he didn't want to go as often as we have in the past. I can accept this change, especially because we do lots of other fun things together. Now I go out dancing with friends, and I've learned a lot of new dance steps that I bring home to show my husband.

If you're a compromiser in your relationship, you won't cultivate your own creative resilience. There are so many more ways than you ever thought to do what you want to do and enjoy your life — and for your partner to do the same.

Your myth-busting tour continues. Enjoy the exhilaration, liberation and empowerment of debunking relationship myths.

103

THE TIME MYTH

Once established, a relationship requires very little time to maintain.

I am constantly amazed at how little time couples spend with each other and how upset they are that they aren't having a wonderful relationship. Some couples haven't been away on their own for a romantic getaway for almost 15 years, and they wonder why they aren't getting along.

Probably you have to work for a living. You have your own interests you'd like to pursue. You have to do housework, run errands, and prepare food. You might be raising children.

There are countless responsibilities that we all have to do on a daily basis. Life can be overwhelming, but being in a relationship is a responsibility, too. Don't take your partner for granted. The rewards of time spent together are manifold.

Each couple determines the percentages that work for them. Some couples want more time together than others. Being together all of the time is just as unhealthy as being apart all of the time. It's guaranteed, however, that as the years roll by, if you're spending less and less meaningful alone time with your partner, your relationship has nowhere to go but downhill.

Busted Myth

Ask yourself: Why is everything else in your life more of a priority than your relationship? Fewer and fewer couples in the United States even have dinner together on a regular basis because they lead such busy lives. Eat together as frequently as you can. Share fun times with each other — only the two of you. Make dates. Have sex. If you don't, your relationship will suffer.

Quality time vs. quantity time. You have to spend a significant amount of time with your partner, just as you have to spend a lot of time with your kids or your friends. Don't fool yourself into thinking that a few moments will do the trick. It won't. You have to devote energy and time to nurturing yourself and your partner, otherwise your connection can't grow. You can't have a thriving relationship if you don't spend time with your partner — just the two of you — more than on birthdays and Valentine's Day.

Never underestimate the power of a romantic getaway — even if you can only afford the time and money for a short time away together. One overnight, only twelve hours, can work wonders. It will rejuvenate you and your partner in countless ways. Trips are always something extra to plan, and they cost money, but they are vital to relationship health. Even if you can only afford to go to your local hotel, have a picnic dinner on your bed. It doesn't have to be a big deal, but it does have to happen and on a regular basis.

Book a quick getaway right now. The only requirement is this: Focus on you and your partner, not on the news, not on your work, and not on your children — just on the two of you. Even if you have some disagreements, don't be afraid to spend this precious time together again and again. The more you go away together, the better it gets.

To find out how to have the best getaway ever, visit my site: **www.lovingforkeeps.com**, then search for "romantic getaway."

If you need to kick-start a getaway, I'll help you with my *Relationship Recharge Getaway* on the Sonoma Coast, California, and I could do it for you virtually anywhere in the world. If you want more details, please visit my website or email me at: mel@lovingforkeeps.com.

Your myth-busting tour continues. Enjoy the exhilaration, liberation and empowerment of debunking relationship myths.

THE INSIGHT MYTH

Insight into issues is what is needed for a relationship to thrive.

Gaining insight into your inner life is important, but if you stay there and don't make the final move to take action to change yourself, you won't get the results you want.

For example, once you admit and recognize that you are being mean to your partner, that realization is not enough. Now you have to do something about it. Are you going to make the necessary changes, or are you going to be self-indulgent and say, "Well, I know I'm that way, and that's the way it is." No one is "that way."

Everyone can be different, especially if they change their behavior because they have the insight to see that their actions have been harmful to themselves and to others.

Busted Myth

Insight is essential, but not the final key that unlocks the door to where you've been hiding out. You can still keep pretending that you don't have to change because you understand yourself intellectually. It doesn't count unless you go to your core. Your gut and your heart, the arenas where your inner self resides, will give you the strength to make a lasting, full-body, visceral change.

Insight to identify a problem is a steppingstone, but sadly, it is the place where most people stop. Don't miss the essential step of confronting yourself. After having the insight, can you change your behaviors and beliefs? Not let yourself off the hook? You have to catch yourself in order to be free. And the barbs on the hook are painful. If there's no pain, no tears, there is no relationship gain.

People who have gone through years of therapy can usually admit that they have various psychological complexes. If they do nothing about them, however, they aren't really any better off than before. They grant themselves excuses and don't take responsibility for themselves. They pay lip service to their partner by lying. If you don't do something with the knowledge you've gained, you're aiding and abetting a relationship crime. It's unconscionable to know something and do nothing about it, but you might need some help from your partner.

Story

One day my husband and I had an argument over what my husband had said at a party. I was indignant and self-righteous over something my husband had done, and all I could do was blame or shame my husband or defend myself. Every statement that came out of my mouth was a blaming, shaming, or a justifying position. I kept accusing him of being inconsiderate and inappropriate. He didn't have much of a reaction. He just sat there. So, instead of getting infuriated by his cool non-reactivity, I kept sitting on the couch for more than half an hour before I could even utter a statement that didn't fall into one of these categories of blame, shame and justification — about myself or my husband. Finally, when I said something about me that was profoundly felt, my husband heard what I had to say. He listened attentively to what I was saying and responded. We ended up having compassion for each other — for the stupid thing that my husband had said and the real thing that was bothering me that had nothing to do with what my husband had done. For both of us, it stirred up our sense of belonging and wanting to be liked. The argument was over. We never talked about it again, no residue to clean or clear up — no pacts made about the future.

❧ ❧ ❧

Beware of righteous indignation; it's taking the high road of morality as a way to inflict shame. If your partner calls you on it, get off your high horse. If you love to pontificate, you might be guilty of this passive-aggressive behavior. Get the insight and then do something to mitigate shame's insidious and destructive qualities within yourself.

If blaming, shaming, and justifying are a way of life for you, which it is for most people, don't be too ashamed to do something about it. Listen to what you are saying to yourself and to your partner.

If your statements can be described by these verbs, you are not confronting yourself and instead are looking for your partner to do all the changing.

Your myth-busting tour continues. Enjoy the exhilaration, liberation and empowerment of debunking relationship myths.

THE FAIRNESS MYTH

Life is fair. My relationship won't break up unless we both agree.

Relationships are life, and life is relationships. Couples don't want to admit that life's natural laws apply to their relationship.

It's not fair that two people can create a relationship, but only one can decide to end it. Yet, don't forget that you can change your relationship unilaterally by changing yourself. There's no need to be in agreement with your partner to make the changes within yourself that you know need to happen.

Busted Myth

You do play a 100-percent role of your half in a relationship. You need to do your inner work, and your partner needs to do the same. Unfortunately, it doesn't mean that you'll definitely find happiness together along the way. Nothing is certain or guaranteed.

Life isn't fair. Relationships aren't fair. It only takes one to break up a relationship, but two to have a successful one. The good news is: You can start to change your relationship on your own.

Once you start changing, the relationship dynamic changes and your partner will probably be forced to change, too. You don't have to wait, but there are never any guarantees. Usually your partner will be surprised and inspired by your personal changes, and she or he will want to meet you at your level of development. But, if your partner refuses to change, then your relationship will continue to be unhappy, intolerable — or will end.

Sometimes some of my students are resentful that they are always the ones to initiate change, and they are tired of being the designated shape-shifter in their relationship. I know when my husband and I have arguments over who is the first one to dig our relationship out of its hole, we disagree about who made the first move. Invariably, he thinks he did, and I think I did. It's a moot point. It really doesn't matter so long as you help each other move forward.

STOP fighting with your partner; fight with yourself. She or he may not do anything toward self-improvement, and that doesn't matter. Go forward on your own. Don't keep waiting to make your move. Do it now. Your partner doesn't have to do anything, but you do. You owe personal transformation to yourself. It is only through personal transformation that your relationship has any hope of changing.

Your myth-busting tour continues. Enjoy the exhilaration, liberation and empowerment of debunking relationship myths.

THE REALITY MYTH

A good relationship requires that partners perceive the world in the same way.

No two people see the world in the same way. Your partner will never see the world as you do. So, stop coercing her or him. A shared reality doesn't exist.

Busted Myth

Trying to change your partner only alleviates the pressure for you to change, which means that neither one of you will. Your marriage cannot improve if there is no change in your thinking. Keep reminding yourself that you and your partner are not from Venus and Mars, but you are two individuals on planet Earth trying to create an expansive relationship that is spacious enough for two complete human beings.

Multiple realities co-exist simultaneously because you and your partner are two separate beings. Two people never see the world in the same way. So, don't expect it. Stop arguing about a shared reality. You don't have the same reality even if you and your partner practice the same religion.

Can't you breathe a sigh of relief knowing that you and your partner aren't supposed to share philosophical and metaphysical worldviews in order to have a thriving relationship?

Story

My husband doesn't like the way I load the dishwasher; it's not systematic enough. He used to get upset, since he thought only his way was the right one. Since he now understands that we can't load the dishwasher the same say, he rarely says anything to me about my inefficient habit. Instead of badgering me, he changed his inner state. He came to a realization that two ways of loading the dishes can co-exist in one household.

My husband does the dishes his way, and I do them my way. It's impossible to agree to an "our way." The dishwasher is no longer the bone of contention that it had been for decades.

🌿 🌿 🌿

What shared-reality bones of contention can you toss out of your relationship? Once you do, you will find much more space where you can live together happily.

Your myth-busting tour continues. Enjoy the exhilaration, liberation and empowerment of debunking relationship myths.

THE HABIT MYTH

I can keep doing what I've always done and my relationship will get better.

People are very attached to their habits and beliefs. They think what they do and think are inviolate, the only way possible for them.

There are billions of people on the planet and billions of belief systems. Which one or ones are right or wrong? If you're a fundamentalist or an extremist, you'll be limited in your thinking. If you can be flexible, more open than rigid, you'll have the capacity to brainstorm and think of ways to enhance your life that are outside the box.

Whatever you espouse, try to think beyond your comfort zones. Your partner challenges you to go in this direction all the time.

Busted Myth

Stop looking in the same old places for the answers to your dilemmas. Be curious and try something new, maybe something you've never tried before. For example, if you've been complaining about your partner for years, try not to, even for a day, and see what happens. If you never get enough sleep, try going to bed earlier, and see what transpires. Experiment until you find what works for you.

If you keep doing the same thing that you've always done, you will NOT get different results. Force yourself to try something else. Change parts or all of your paradigm. If what you're thinking and doing aren't helping your relationship, then try other avenues. If those don't work, do something else. The possibilities are infinite.

Story

Sex in a long-term relationship is emotionally risky. In the past when my husband and I used to have sex, we didn't talk much. Once we'd decide to make love, our verbal communication would turn off. We weren't willing to take the risk of saying something in case we offended each other and ruined the romantic moment. Now we start and stop sex by telling each other what we like and don't like, sharing our creative ideas. Our willingness to be more vulnerable has immeasurably enhanced our sex life. Due to this one change, we've infused our sex life with more laughter, fun, play — and depth.

❧ ❧ ❧

Can you be flexible and still maintain your integrity? Yes! You could give up all of your beliefs and live a different kind of life and still have an identity and know who you are.

If you're still not convinced that you can change your beliefs, read my blog post on meaning flexibility.

(Go to: **www.lovingforkeeps.com**, then search for "meaning flexibility.")

Your myth-busting tour continues. Enjoy the exhilaration, liberation and empowerment of debunking relationship myths.

THE TRUST MYTH

A good relationship is with someone I trust and who makes me feel safe.

Couples talk about trust and safety issues because they don't have boundaries, which means they don't have a secure sense of who they are. The more you know who you are, what you'll tolerate, and what you won't, no one, not even your partner, will violate the parameters of your personal space.

You can eliminate mixed messages in your relationship by being clear about what works for you and what doesn't. Do you say NO when you mean YES and vice versa? And if you don't know, can you say that you don't?

You have a right to your own values and opinions. And you have a right to change them because you're an evolving human being.

Stand your ground, not defiantly against your partner, but as a way to define yourself. Don't let anyone take advantage of you physically, sexually, or emotionally — not your partner, not anyone.

You radiate your boundaries from the inside of who you are. Walls you arbitrarily construct around you will collapse under pressure if you don't cultivate your own inner strength.

Busted Myth

Your partner will hurt you emotionally. You can't put up barriers against pain. And you will lash out to emotionally wound your partner, offensively and defensively. Be careful of the word "boundaries" because the metaphor is more about contraction and setting limits than expansion and growing — which is life's goal.

Physical safety has to exist for a relationship to flourish, but emotional safety doesn't, except inside yourself. Relationships are messy, risky, and dangerous. You have to be the person you trust. Trust in your partner is regularly broken and continually rebuilt. Cultivate belief and trust in yourself and bring a resilient self to your relationship. That's the only way to be safe, but it is no guarantee against being hurt.

When you go out every day, how do you greet the world? With fear, trepidation, and pessimism, or love, light, and optimism? Open up your heart to all that is possible, but never lose yourself and forget who you are.

Your myth-busting tour continues. Enjoy the exhilaration, liberation and empowerment of debunking relationship myths.

THE RELATIONSHIP MYTH

A relationship has an existence all its own beyond the two partners.

Couples often refer to their relationship as a real thing that they need to work on. It's not possible, because a relationship is not a separate thing apart from its two participants.

You need to understand how your relationship operates and how you can respond when you're conscious of what's happening. Refer to the Something Feels Wrong Myth to review relationship dynamics.

All long-term relationships evolve in the same way. Some people can't get past the honeymoon phase and decide to keep changing partners because they are so addicted to the rush of infatuation.

You will never be happy unless you learn how to appreciate all of the stages that keep cycling in a relationship, just as you do when you're raising children. The idyllic, euphoric infant stage doesn't last for long. Your baby needs to grow up, and so do you. And, as your baby grows up, you need help understanding childhood development. As your relationship matures, you need long-term relationship education.

Anytime my husband and I sit down and have a serious discussion about how we can work on our relationship, we don't know how, unless it is predicated on an agreement that, once made, we can't keep. Yes, we can agree to go on more getaways and more dates — that's something we do have to agree on, but how to fix or repair our relationship to make it what we want never gets results. Why not? Because we both have different visions for it. The only thing we realize we can agree and commit to is having a vibrant, thriving, successful relationship — whatever that means to each one of us.

For example, my husband thinks that part of a relationship is watching movies together. I don't enjoy watching movies or TV series as much as my husband does. On the other hand, I like reading out loud together, and my husband enjoys it, but he isn't willing to engage in this activity as often as I would like. My husband dreams of "petting" on the couch and looking at a screen while I dream of seducing each other with our voices. We'll never be able to agree on which activity is better than the other. Instead of getting resentful, we must remember that we're two people with different ideas about what would make a relationship ideal.

How can you handle this constraint of loving to do different things? First of all, you'll never find someone who has the same level of motivation to do exactly the same thing at the same time you want to.

Couples feel that this is the definition of true compatibility. It's not. Even Siamese twins don't have that kind of symbiotic relationship. (Read the fascinating true story of *Chang and Eng* by Darin Straus where one of the twins was an alcoholic and the other a teetotaler!)

Busted Myth

Relationships are not possible to work on. You can only work on yourself — not on your partner, not on your relationship. The relationship doesn't exist apart from you and your partner. It is not a third entity. The connection between you and your partner cannot improve unless you work on yourself, and your partner does the same.

The system of marriage is working on my husband and me in this way: Our relationship is telling us that we're two completely distinct people, that we have a right to our likes and dislikes and what we want to do with our lives, but we do like sharing each other's lives, as well. And, we can share without compromising ourselves.

When you want to please your partner, you're not just giving in or settling for something that you don't want. Don't watch films when you don't want to. Don't read out loud when you don't want to. Do those activities when you want to be generous, when you want to give your partner a gift of her or his choice for which you ask nothing in return. You're offering your partner something that you know will make her or him happy. It's not about you — it's about a no-strings-attached present.

Don't follow in the footsteps of Homer Simpson who buys Marge a bowling ball for her birthday when she doesn't like bowling. He's a clueless husband who is just being selfish. We laugh at him because we all have his same foibles.

To not be like Homer, you need to self-reflect and self-confront. Be vigilant and remember this quote:

"To grow mature is to separate more distinctly, to connect more closely…" — *Hugo von Hofmannsthal (1874-1929)*.

Your myth-busting tour continues. Enjoy the exhilaration, liberation and empowerment of debunking relationship myths.

THE FAIRYTALE MYTH

A good relationship must be like something out of a fairytale.

After more than 35 years of marriage, I am still humbled by what I don't understand — both about myself and my own marriage.

Every book and every website will pretend that there's an answer, a way around the pain. Don't believe them. You'll only hit challenges, one after another. Sometimes you'll know what to do; sometimes you won't.

Everyone, no matter the cultural background, holds the fairytale myth dear to her or his heart. I'm not deriding your yearnings (because I have them myself), but I do ask you to question them. It's in our DNA. We've been spoon-fed the fairytale ideals since childhood. Santa Claus epitomizes generosity, but to grow up we had to stop believing in his sled and flying reindeer.

Busted Myth

Marriage, a long-term relationship, is the most challenging relationship I've ever had — more so than my relationships with my parents, my siblings, and my son. At times I felt I was going crazy, even after years of studying different ways of looking at my marital issues. No approach guaranteed the results I hoped for or wanted until my husband and I read Dr. David Schnarch's *Passionate Marriage*, the most important relationship book, along with mine, that you ever need to study. Dr. Schnarch turned our relationship right side up, made us face reality, and helped us give up our childish beliefs in fairytales.

You'll never reach a state of nirvana that can be sustained. This is a fairytale. You won't always be happy, but you'll be real. This is what my book can help you with — getting real — which doesn't mean perfect. Time after time the long-term relationship journey will bring you to your knees, both in suffering and gratitude. It's time to get rid of wishful thinking of a magical panacea.

Consider this scenario: Just when you think you're on top of the world, one evening you come home to find something that your partner did that sets your relationship into a tailspin before you even know what hits you. You blame her or him and vice versa. You feel powerless. Does this scenario sound familiar?

Variations on the above continue happening until the day you die because you can't control anyone or any situation. When you can't find a place of calm within yourself, you may forget what you've been studying and learning about your relationship. After all, you're only human. Nobody lives in a vacuum, and everyone becomes overwhelmed. That's how life works. If anyone or any program promises you otherwise, they are lying.

The only thing to strive for is this: Cultivate your relationship with yourself. It's the one that counts in the end — not the fairytale relationship of Prince and Princess Charming. If Cinderella didn't love herself, she wouldn't be able to love her dream husband. If the same weren't true about Prince Charming, he wouldn't be able to love his glass-slippered wife. They are archetypal storybook characters. You are human, and ever so much more interesting because you're real.

Your myth-busting tour concludes!

CONCLUSION

What's in a myth?

These 31 pernicious myths are very hard to overcome. Recognize the power they have over you. Change your thinking about each lie, even if it feels counter-intuitive and/or counterculture to do so. Only by understanding the truth will you be set free to have an extraordinary relationship with your partner. Believing in myths is damaging to you and your relationship because they don't help you face reality. They are not benign; they actually are at the root of much unhappiness. That's why eradicating them one by one from your belief system is absolutely essential.

As John F. Kennedy stated in a 1962 commencement address at Yale University:

> *"The great enemy of the truth is very often not the lie – deliberate, contrived and dishonest – but the myth – persistent, persuasive, and unrealistic."*

My husband and I almost got divorced after 25 years of marriage. Why? Not because we weren't meant for each other or our relationship was over, but because we didn't understand how a long-term relationship works. Our ignorance almost deprived us of the extraordinary part that was yet to come.

Relationship dynamics drive couples to valleys. It is possible to climb back up to the peaks again and again, if you lighten your heavy load of carrying these 31 deadly myths around in your belief backpack.

131

ABOUT MELISSA SMITH BAKER

I am a relationship blogger, trainer, and author. I teach relationship classes and have helped hundreds of people by not giving them tips and techniques, but by presenting new ways of understanding the following concepts: love, commitment, relationship dynamics, personal growth, stress, intimacy, sex, desire, self care, freedom, and connection.

I believe in the infinite ingenuity of humankind. You are the one who can figure out how to live your life by incorporating what works for you, in your own unique way. May what I've presented spark your imagination and be a springboard for your creativity. May you be happier and more fulfilled by becoming the best person you can be — for you and for your partner.

NOTES

14 Contrary to popular belief, soul mates are not found: Dr. Helen. 12/14/12. www.pjmedia.com: *Those Who Believe In Soul Mates Are Found To Be 150 Percent More Likely To End Up Divorced.*

18 Having it all is an illusion: Ray Dalio. www.bwater.com. 2011. *Principles.*

18 They are choices between one anxiety and another: David Schnarch. 1997. *Passionate Marriage.* New York: Henry Holt and Company, p. 297.

25 If you don't regulate the stress that is going on: Melody Beattie. 1992. *Codependent No More.* Minnesota: Hazelden and David Allen. 2001. *Getting Things Done: The Art of Stress-Free Productivity.* New York: Penguin.

29 You aren't your feelings: 12/03/09.www.psychologytoday.com: *How Not To Be A Victim of Your Emotions.*

30 Don't ask your partner to manage your state: Melody Beattie. 1992. *Codependent No More.* Minnesota: Hazelden.

31 A committed relationship is learning how to sail your own boat: Murray Bowen. www.vermontcenterforfamilystudies.org. *Eight Concepts of Bowen Theory* and David Schnarch. 1997. *Passionate Marriage.* New York: Henry Holt and Company, p. 109.

35 A long-term partner actually becomes more important: David Schnarch. 2009. *Intimacy and Desire.* New York: Beaufort, p. 170 and Murray Bowen. www.ideastoaction.wordpress.com/dr-bowen.

41 When this happens, take heart: David Schnarch. 1997. *Passionate Marriage.* New York: Henry Holt and Company. For more on depathologizing long-term relationships, read this book.

47 If you weren't equal: Murray Bowen. www.interventions.net/bowentheoryupdated and Daniel Siegel. 2001. *The Developing Mind: How Relationships and the Brain Interact to Shape Who We Are.* Guilford.

56 Responsible adults are not abandoned or victims in relationships: David Schnarch. 1997. *Passionate Marriage.* New York: Henry Holt and Company and Tal Ben-Shahar. 2010. *Even Happier: A Gratitude Journal for Daily Joy and Lasting Fulfillment.* New York:

Melissa Smith Baker

McGraw Hill and John Bradshaw. 2005. *Healing The Shame That Binds You*. Florida: Health Communications.

59 It's only natural that you might not want to admit that you have vindictive feelings: Iris Krasnow. 01/25/12. www.huffingtonpost.com: *Help! I Hate My Husband*.

60 People who can't acknowledge that they feel hate: David Schnarch. 1997. *Passionate Marriage*. New York: Henry Holt and Company, p. 310.

67 Taking care of yourself is your number one priority: Melody Beattie. 1992. *Codependent No More*. Minnesota: Hazelden, p. 114.

68 Because if you don't, you'll want to control your partner: Melody Beattie. 1992. *Codependent No More*. Minnesota: Hazelden, p. 36.

73 A half-million years ago: Helen Fisher. 1994. *Anatomy of Love: A Natural History of Mating, Marriage, and Why We Stray*. New York. Ballantine.

74 Genital and sexual primes are different: David Schnarch. 1997. *Passionate Marriage*. New York: Henry Holt and Company.

77 There's supposed to be a higher and lower desire partner: David Schnarch.2009. *Intimacy and Desire*. New York: Beaufort, pp. 9-19.

91 It takes a neocortex to do this: Helen Fisher. 1994. *Anatomy of Love: A Natural History of Mating, Marriage, and Why We Stray*. New York, Ballantine.

92 Intimacy with your partner, however, doesn't have a linear trajectory: David Schnarch. 1997. *Passionate Marriage*. New York: Henry Holt and Company, pp. 100-107 and Esther Perel. 2007. *Mating In Captivity: Unlocking Erotic Intelligence*. New York: Harper, p. 29.

95 You and your partner are always communicating: David Schnarch. 1997. *Passionate Marriage*. New York: Henry Holt and Company, p. 101.

102 If a relationship with your partner is worth more than the relationship with yourself: David Schnarch. 1997. *Passionate Marriage*. New York: Henry Holt and Company and David Whyte. 2009. *The Three Marriages: Re-imagining Work, Self and Relationship*. New York: Riverhead.

103 If you're a compromiser in your relationship, you won't cultivate your own creative resilience: Daniel Siegel. www.soundstruc.com. *The Mindful Brain*.

CONNECT WITH ME

Website:
http://www.lovingforkeeps.com

Google +:
https://plus.google.com/108333386190421870729/posts

Pinterest:
http://pinterest.com/lovingforkeeps/

LinkedIn:
http://www.linkedin.com/company/loving-for-keeps/

Facebook:
https://www.facebook.com/LovingForKeeps

Twitter:
https://twitter.com/lovingforkeeps

Email:
mel@lovingforkeeps.com

Telephone:
707-827-1660
Sebastopol, California

Printed in Great Britain
by Amazon

23650482R00081